50 Premium Mustard Recipes

By: Kelly Johnson

Table of Contents

- Honey Mustard Chicken
- Mustard Glazed Salmon
- Dijon Mustard Chicken
- Spicy Mustard BBQ Sauce
- Mustard-Marinated Steak
- Mustard Vinaigrette Salad Dressing
- Roasted Mustard Brussels Sprouts
- Mustard-Rosemary Roasted Potatoes
- Mustard and Herb Crusted Pork Tenderloin
- Mustard and Dill Potato Salad
- Mustard Baked Salmon
- Mustard-Crusted Chicken Thighs
- Grilled Mustard Shrimp Skewers
- Mustard and Garlic Roasted Carrots
- Sweet Mustard Glazed Chicken Wings
- Dijon Mustard Deviled Eggs
- Mustard Cream Sauce for Steaks
- Mustard Braised Pork Belly
- Mustard-Pickle Coleslaw
- Mustard and Caper Fish Fillets
- Mustard-Maple Glazed Ham
- Creamy Mustard and Spinach Pasta
- Mustard-Sesame Dressing
- Mustard-Lemon Chicken Skewers
- Mustard and Herb Roasted Lamb
- Mustard and Bacon Brussels Sprouts
- Spicy Mustard Pickles
- Honey Mustard Grilled Veggies
- Mustard Potatoes with Garlic and Thyme
- Mustard Chicken Salad
- Mustard-Cranberry Sauce
- Mustard and Bacon Mac and Cheese
- Hot Mustard Pork Tacos
- Mustard-Cabbage Stir-Fry
- Dijon Mustard and Roasted Beet Salad

- Mustard and Walnut-Crusted Fish
- Mustard Garlic Roasted Chicken
- Mustard Glazed Asparagus
- Mustard and Apple Coleslaw
- Mustard-Dill Marinated Cucumbers
- Mustard and Herb Marinated Chicken Breasts
- Honey Mustard Salmon Burgers
- Mustard and Apricot Glazed Ribs
- Mustard Spiced Roasted Sweet Potatoes
- Mustard and Chive Creamed Spinach
- Mustard and Bacon-Sautéed Green Beans
- Mustard and Onion Baked Potatoes
- Mustard-Maple Roasted Squash
- Mustard-Cream Sauce for Roasted Veggies
- Dijon Mustard and Mushroom Gravy

Mustard Chicken

Ingredients:

- 4 chicken breasts
- 2 tablespoons Dijon mustard
- 1 tablespoon honey
- 1 tablespoon olive oil
- 2 cloves garlic, minced
- 1 teaspoon dried thyme
- Salt and pepper to taste

Instructions:

1. Preheat your oven to 375°F (190°C).
2. In a bowl, mix Dijon mustard, honey, olive oil, garlic, thyme, salt, and pepper.
3. Coat the chicken breasts with the mustard mixture.
4. Place the chicken on a baking sheet and bake for 25-30 minutes or until the chicken reaches an internal temperature of 165°F (74°C).
5. Serve with your favorite side dishes.

Mustard Glazed Salmon

Ingredients:

- 4 salmon fillets
- 2 tablespoons Dijon mustard
- 1 tablespoon honey
- 1 tablespoon olive oil
- 1 tablespoon lemon juice
- Salt and pepper to taste

Instructions:

1. Preheat the oven to 375°F (190°C).
2. In a small bowl, mix Dijon mustard, honey, olive oil, lemon juice, salt, and pepper.
3. Place the salmon fillets on a baking sheet lined with parchment paper.
4. Brush the mustard glaze generously over the salmon fillets.
5. Bake for 12-15 minutes or until the salmon is cooked through and flakes easily with a fork.
6. Serve immediately.

Dijon Mustard Chicken

Ingredients:

- 4 chicken thighs (bone-in or boneless)
- 2 tablespoons Dijon mustard
- 1 tablespoon olive oil
- 2 tablespoons white wine vinegar
- 1 teaspoon fresh thyme
- Salt and pepper to taste

Instructions:

1. Preheat your oven to 375°F (190°C).
2. Mix Dijon mustard, olive oil, white wine vinegar, thyme, salt, and pepper in a bowl.
3. Coat the chicken thighs with the mustard marinade and let them sit for 10 minutes.
4. Place the chicken on a baking sheet and bake for 30-35 minutes or until fully cooked.
5. Serve with a side of roasted vegetables.

Spicy Mustard BBQ Sauce

Ingredients:

- 1/2 cup Dijon mustard
- 1/4 cup apple cider vinegar
- 1/4 cup honey
- 1/4 cup ketchup
- 2 tablespoons hot sauce
- 1 teaspoon smoked paprika
- Salt and pepper to taste

Instructions:

1. In a saucepan, combine Dijon mustard, apple cider vinegar, honey, ketchup, hot sauce, and smoked paprika.
2. Bring to a simmer over medium heat, stirring occasionally.
3. Let the sauce simmer for about 10-15 minutes until it thickens slightly.
4. Adjust seasoning with salt and pepper.
5. Serve as a dipping sauce for grilled meats or as a glaze.

Mustard-Marinated Steak

Ingredients:

- 2 rib-eye steaks
- 3 tablespoons Dijon mustard
- 1 tablespoon olive oil
- 2 cloves garlic, minced
- 1 tablespoon fresh rosemary, chopped
- Salt and pepper to taste

Instructions:

1. In a bowl, whisk together Dijon mustard, olive oil, garlic, rosemary, salt, and pepper.
2. Coat the steaks with the marinade and refrigerate for at least 30 minutes (or overnight for more flavor).
3. Preheat your grill or pan to medium-high heat.
4. Grill the steaks for 4-5 minutes per side for medium-rare, or until your desired doneness.
5. Let the steaks rest for a few minutes before serving.

Mustard Vinaigrette Salad Dressing

Ingredients:

- 2 tablespoons Dijon mustard
- 1 tablespoon red wine vinegar
- 1/4 cup olive oil
- 1 teaspoon honey (optional)
- Salt and pepper to taste

Instructions:

1. In a small bowl, whisk together Dijon mustard, red wine vinegar, honey (if using), salt, and pepper.
2. Slowly whisk in olive oil until the dressing emulsifies and thickens.
3. Pour over your favorite salad greens and toss to coat.

Roasted Mustard Brussels Sprouts

Ingredients:

- 1 lb Brussels sprouts, trimmed and halved
- 2 tablespoons Dijon mustard
- 1 tablespoon olive oil
- 1 tablespoon honey
- 1 teaspoon garlic powder
- Salt and pepper to taste

Instructions:

1. Preheat the oven to 400°F (200°C).
2. In a bowl, whisk together Dijon mustard, olive oil, honey, garlic powder, salt, and pepper.
3. Toss the Brussels sprouts with the mustard mixture until they are well coated.
4. Spread them out on a baking sheet and roast for 20-25 minutes, shaking the pan halfway through.
5. Serve immediately.

Mustard-Rosemary Roasted Potatoes

Ingredients:

- 2 lbs baby potatoes, halved
- 2 tablespoons Dijon mustard
- 1 tablespoon olive oil
- 2 tablespoons fresh rosemary, chopped
- 1 teaspoon garlic powder
- Salt and pepper to taste

Instructions:

1. Preheat your oven to 425°F (220°C).
2. In a bowl, mix Dijon mustard, olive oil, rosemary, garlic powder, salt, and pepper.
3. Toss the potatoes with the mustard mixture until they are evenly coated.
4. Spread the potatoes on a baking sheet and roast for 30-35 minutes or until golden brown and crispy.
5. Serve hot.

Mustard and Herb Crusted Pork Tenderloin

Ingredients:

- 1 pork tenderloin (about 1 lb)
- 2 tablespoons Dijon mustard
- 1 tablespoon olive oil
- 2 tablespoons fresh parsley, chopped
- 1 tablespoon fresh thyme, chopped
- 1 teaspoon garlic powder
- Salt and pepper to taste

Instructions:

1. Preheat the oven to 375°F (190°C).
2. In a small bowl, mix Dijon mustard, olive oil, parsley, thyme, garlic powder, salt, and pepper.
3. Rub the mustard mixture all over the pork tenderloin.
4. Place the tenderloin on a baking sheet and roast for 25-30 minutes or until it reaches an internal temperature of 145°F (63°C).
5. Let the pork rest for 5-10 minutes before slicing and serving.

Mustard and Dill Potato Salad

Ingredients:

- 1.5 lbs baby potatoes, boiled and halved
- 2 tablespoons Dijon mustard
- 1/4 cup sour cream
- 1/4 cup mayonnaise
- 1 tablespoon apple cider vinegar
- 2 tablespoons fresh dill, chopped
- Salt and pepper to taste

Instructions:

1. In a large bowl, mix the Dijon mustard, sour cream, mayonnaise, apple cider vinegar, fresh dill, salt, and pepper.
2. Add the boiled potatoes and gently toss to coat.
3. Refrigerate for at least 30 minutes before serving for the flavors to meld together.
4. Serve chilled.

Mustard Baked Salmon

Ingredients:

- 4 salmon fillets
- 3 tablespoons Dijon mustard
- 1 tablespoon honey
- 1 tablespoon olive oil
- 1 tablespoon lemon juice
- Salt and pepper to taste

Instructions:

1. Preheat the oven to 375°F (190°C).
2. In a small bowl, whisk together Dijon mustard, honey, olive oil, lemon juice, salt, and pepper.
3. Place the salmon fillets on a baking sheet lined with parchment paper.
4. Brush the mustard mixture generously over the fillets.
5. Bake for 12-15 minutes or until the salmon flakes easily with a fork.
6. Serve with roasted vegetables or a fresh salad.

Mustard-Crusted Chicken Thighs

Ingredients:

- 4 bone-in, skin-on chicken thighs
- 3 tablespoons Dijon mustard
- 1 tablespoon olive oil
- 1 teaspoon garlic powder
- 1 teaspoon dried rosemary
- Salt and pepper to taste

Instructions:

1. Preheat the oven to 400°F (200°C).
2. In a small bowl, mix Dijon mustard, olive oil, garlic powder, rosemary, salt, and pepper.
3. Rub the mustard mixture over the chicken thighs, coating them evenly.
4. Place the chicken thighs on a baking sheet and bake for 35-40 minutes or until the chicken reaches an internal temperature of 165°F (74°C).
5. Serve with a side of roasted potatoes or steamed vegetables.

Grilled Mustard Shrimp Skewers

Ingredients:

- 1 lb large shrimp, peeled and deveined
- 3 tablespoons Dijon mustard
- 1 tablespoon olive oil
- 1 tablespoon lemon juice
- 1 teaspoon smoked paprika
- 1 garlic clove, minced
- Salt and pepper to taste
- Wooden skewers (soaked in water for 30 minutes)

Instructions:

1. Preheat the grill to medium-high heat.
2. In a bowl, combine Dijon mustard, olive oil, lemon juice, smoked paprika, garlic, salt, and pepper.
3. Toss the shrimp in the mustard mixture, ensuring they are well coated.
4. Thread the shrimp onto the soaked skewers.
5. Grill the shrimp for 2-3 minutes on each side, or until pink and cooked through.
6. Serve with a drizzle of extra mustard sauce.

Mustard and Garlic Roasted Carrots

Ingredients:

- 1 lb carrots, peeled and cut into sticks
- 2 tablespoons Dijon mustard
- 1 tablespoon olive oil
- 2 garlic cloves, minced
- 1 tablespoon honey
- Salt and pepper to taste

Instructions:

1. Preheat the oven to 400°F (200°C).
2. In a bowl, whisk together Dijon mustard, olive oil, garlic, honey, salt, and pepper.
3. Toss the carrot sticks in the mustard mixture until coated.
4. Spread the carrots on a baking sheet in a single layer.
5. Roast for 20-25 minutes or until the carrots are tender and lightly caramelized.
6. Serve as a side dish with grilled meats or roasted chicken.

Sweet Mustard Glazed Chicken Wings

Ingredients:

- 12 chicken wings, trimmed
- 3 tablespoons Dijon mustard
- 2 tablespoons honey
- 1 tablespoon soy sauce
- 1 tablespoon apple cider vinegar
- 1/2 teaspoon smoked paprika
- Salt and pepper to taste

Instructions:

1. Preheat your oven to 400°F (200°C).
2. In a bowl, whisk together Dijon mustard, honey, soy sauce, apple cider vinegar, smoked paprika, salt, and pepper.
3. Toss the chicken wings in the mustard glaze until they are fully coated.
4. Place the wings on a baking sheet lined with parchment paper.
5. Bake for 25-30 minutes, flipping halfway, until the wings are golden and crispy.
6. Serve with your favorite dipping sauce.

Dijon Mustard Deviled Eggs

Ingredients:

- 6 hard-boiled eggs, peeled and halved
- 3 tablespoons mayonnaise
- 2 tablespoons Dijon mustard
- 1 teaspoon white vinegar
- 1 teaspoon Dijon mustard for garnish
- Salt and pepper to taste
- Paprika for garnish

Instructions:

1. Slice the hard-boiled eggs in half and remove the yolks.
2. Mash the yolks in a bowl and mix with mayonnaise, Dijon mustard, vinegar, salt, and pepper until smooth.
3. Spoon or pipe the yolk mixture back into the egg whites.
4. Garnish with a small dot of Dijon mustard and a sprinkle of paprika.
5. Chill in the refrigerator until ready to serve.

Mustard Cream Sauce for Steaks

Ingredients:

- 1 tablespoon olive oil
- 1/2 cup heavy cream
- 2 tablespoons Dijon mustard
- 1 tablespoon white wine
- 1 teaspoon fresh thyme
- Salt and pepper to taste

Instructions:

1. In a skillet, heat olive oil over medium heat.
2. Add the heavy cream, Dijon mustard, white wine, thyme, salt, and pepper.
3. Stir and bring to a simmer. Let it cook for 2-3 minutes until the sauce thickens.
4. Pour the mustard cream sauce over your grilled or pan-seared steak.
5. Serve immediately.

Mustard Braised Pork Belly

Ingredients:

- 1 lb pork belly, cut into 2-inch pieces
- 3 tablespoons Dijon mustard
- 1/2 cup white wine
- 1 tablespoon olive oil
- 1 teaspoon garlic, minced
- 1/2 cup chicken broth
- 1 tablespoon fresh thyme
- Salt and pepper to taste

Instructions:

1. In a heavy-bottomed pot, heat olive oil over medium-high heat.
2. Season the pork belly pieces with salt and pepper, and sear them in the pot until browned on all sides.
3. Add the garlic and cook for another minute.
4. Stir in Dijon mustard, white wine, chicken broth, and thyme.
5. Bring to a simmer, cover, and braise for 1.5-2 hours or until the pork is tender and cooked through.
6. Serve with mashed potatoes or roasted vegetables.

Mustard-Pickle Coleslaw

Ingredients:

- 4 cups shredded cabbage
- 1 cup shredded carrots
- 1/4 cup pickle relish
- 2 tablespoons Dijon mustard
- 1/4 cup mayonnaise
- 1 tablespoon apple cider vinegar
- 1 tablespoon honey
- Salt and pepper to taste

Instructions:

1. In a large bowl, combine shredded cabbage, carrots, and pickle relish.
2. In a separate bowl, whisk together Dijon mustard, mayonnaise, apple cider vinegar, honey, salt, and pepper.
3. Pour the dressing over the cabbage mixture and toss to combine.
4. Refrigerate for at least 1 hour before serving for the flavors to meld together.
5. Serve chilled as a side dish.

Mustard and Caper Fish Fillets

Ingredients:

- 4 fish fillets (such as cod or tilapia)
- 2 tablespoons Dijon mustard
- 1 tablespoon olive oil
- 2 tablespoons capers, drained and chopped
- 1 tablespoon fresh lemon juice
- Salt and pepper to taste
- Fresh parsley for garnish

Instructions:

1. Preheat the oven to 375°F (190°C).
2. In a small bowl, mix Dijon mustard, olive oil, capers, lemon juice, salt, and pepper.
3. Place the fish fillets on a baking sheet lined with parchment paper.
4. Spread the mustard mixture evenly over the fish fillets.
5. Bake for 12-15 minutes, or until the fish flakes easily with a fork.
6. Garnish with fresh parsley and serve with roasted vegetables or a salad.

Mustard-Maple Glazed Ham

Ingredients:

- 1 fully cooked ham (about 5 lbs)
- 1/4 cup Dijon mustard
- 1/4 cup pure maple syrup
- 2 tablespoons brown sugar
- 1 tablespoon apple cider vinegar
- 1/2 teaspoon ground cinnamon
- Salt and pepper to taste

Instructions:

1. Preheat the oven to 350°F (175°C).
2. In a bowl, whisk together Dijon mustard, maple syrup, brown sugar, apple cider vinegar, cinnamon, salt, and pepper.
3. Place the ham on a roasting rack in a large baking dish.
4. Brush the ham with the mustard-maple glaze.
5. Roast for 1.5-2 hours, basting every 30 minutes, until the ham reaches an internal temperature of 140°F (60°C).
6. Let the ham rest for 10 minutes before slicing. Serve with mashed potatoes or roasted vegetables.

Creamy Mustard and Spinach Pasta

Ingredients:

- 12 oz pasta (penne or fusilli works well)
- 2 tablespoons Dijon mustard
- 1 cup heavy cream
- 2 cups fresh spinach, chopped
- 1 tablespoon olive oil
- 1/2 cup grated Parmesan cheese
- Salt and pepper to taste

Instructions:

1. Cook the pasta according to package directions. Drain and set aside.
2. In a large skillet, heat olive oil over medium heat. Add the spinach and sauté until wilted.
3. Stir in Dijon mustard and heavy cream, cooking for 3-4 minutes until the sauce thickens.
4. Add the cooked pasta to the skillet, tossing to coat the pasta in the sauce.
5. Stir in Parmesan cheese and season with salt and pepper.
6. Serve warm with additional Parmesan on top.

Mustard-Sesame Dressing

Ingredients:

- 3 tablespoons Dijon mustard
- 1 tablespoon sesame oil
- 1 tablespoon olive oil
- 2 teaspoons soy sauce
- 1 tablespoon rice vinegar
- 1 teaspoon honey
- 1/2 teaspoon sesame seeds
- Salt and pepper to taste

Instructions:

1. In a small bowl, whisk together Dijon mustard, sesame oil, olive oil, soy sauce, rice vinegar, honey, sesame seeds, salt, and pepper.
2. Drizzle the dressing over salads, roasted vegetables, or grilled meats.
3. Serve immediately or refrigerate for later use.

Mustard-Lemon Chicken Skewers

Ingredients:

- 2 lbs chicken breast, cut into 1-inch cubes
- 2 tablespoons Dijon mustard
- 1 tablespoon olive oil
- 2 tablespoons fresh lemon juice
- 1 teaspoon lemon zest
- 2 garlic cloves, minced
- Salt and pepper to taste
- Wooden skewers (soaked in water for 30 minutes)

Instructions:

1. In a bowl, mix Dijon mustard, olive oil, lemon juice, lemon zest, garlic, salt, and pepper.
2. Add the chicken cubes and toss to coat evenly. Marinate for at least 30 minutes.
3. Thread the marinated chicken onto soaked skewers.
4. Grill the skewers over medium-high heat for 5-7 minutes on each side, or until the chicken is fully cooked.
5. Serve with a side of rice or a fresh salad.

Mustard and Herb Roasted Lamb

Ingredients:

- 4 lamb chops
- 2 tablespoons Dijon mustard
- 1 tablespoon fresh rosemary, chopped
- 1 tablespoon fresh thyme, chopped
- 2 cloves garlic, minced
- 2 tablespoons olive oil
- Salt and pepper to taste

Instructions:

1. Preheat the oven to 400°F (200°C).
2. In a small bowl, mix Dijon mustard, rosemary, thyme, garlic, olive oil, salt, and pepper.
3. Rub the mustard-herb mixture over the lamb chops.
4. Roast the lamb chops for 20-25 minutes, depending on desired doneness.
5. Serve with roasted potatoes or a mint yogurt sauce.

Mustard and Bacon Brussels Sprouts

Ingredients:

- 1 lb Brussels sprouts, trimmed and halved
- 4 slices bacon, chopped
- 2 tablespoons Dijon mustard
- 1 tablespoon maple syrup
- 1 tablespoon olive oil
- Salt and pepper to taste

Instructions:

1. Preheat the oven to 400°F (200°C).
2. In a skillet, cook the bacon over medium heat until crispy. Remove and set aside.
3. In a small bowl, whisk together Dijon mustard, maple syrup, olive oil, salt, and pepper.
4. Toss the Brussels sprouts in the mustard mixture and arrange them on a baking sheet.
5. Roast for 20-25 minutes, stirring halfway through.
6. Top with the crispy bacon before serving.

Spicy Mustard Pickles

Ingredients:

- 4 cups cucumber slices
- 1/2 cup Dijon mustard
- 1/4 cup white vinegar
- 2 tablespoons sugar
- 1 tablespoon chili flakes
- 1 teaspoon garlic powder
- Salt and pepper to taste

Instructions:

1. In a bowl, combine the cucumber slices, Dijon mustard, white vinegar, sugar, chili flakes, garlic powder, salt, and pepper.
2. Toss the cucumbers until well coated.
3. Let the pickles sit in the refrigerator for at least 2 hours to allow the flavors to develop.
4. Serve as a tangy, spicy side or snack.

Honey Mustard Grilled Veggies

Ingredients:

- 2 cups mixed vegetables (zucchini, bell peppers, onions, etc.)
- 3 tablespoons Dijon mustard
- 1 tablespoon honey
- 1 tablespoon olive oil
- 1 tablespoon lemon juice
- Salt and pepper to taste

Instructions:

1. Preheat the grill to medium-high heat.
2. In a small bowl, whisk together Dijon mustard, honey, olive oil, lemon juice, salt, and pepper.
3. Toss the vegetables in the mustard mixture until evenly coated.
4. Grill the vegetables for 5-7 minutes per side, or until tender and slightly charred.
5. Serve hot as a side dish or topping for salads.

Mustard Potatoes with Garlic and Thyme

Ingredients:

- 4 cups baby potatoes, halved
- 2 tablespoons Dijon mustard
- 1 tablespoon olive oil
- 2 cloves garlic, minced
- 1 tablespoon fresh thyme, chopped
- Salt and pepper to taste

Instructions:

1. Preheat the oven to 400°F (200°C).
2. In a bowl, combine Dijon mustard, olive oil, garlic, thyme, salt, and pepper.
3. Toss the halved potatoes in the mustard mixture until well coated.
4. Spread the potatoes on a baking sheet and roast for 25-30 minutes, or until golden and crispy.
5. Serve as a side dish with roasted meats or grilled fish.

Mustard Chicken Salad

Ingredients:

- 2 cooked chicken breasts, shredded
- 2 tablespoons Dijon mustard
- 1 tablespoon mayonnaise
- 1 tablespoon apple cider vinegar
- 1 tablespoon honey
- 1/2 cup diced celery
- 1/4 cup chopped red onion
- Salt and pepper to taste

Instructions:

1. In a bowl, whisk together Dijon mustard, mayonnaise, apple cider vinegar, honey, salt, and pepper.
2. Add the shredded chicken, celery, and red onion to the bowl and toss to combine.
3. Refrigerate for 30 minutes before serving.
4. Serve the chicken salad on a bed of greens or as a sandwich.

Mustard-Cranberry Sauce

Ingredients:

- 1 cup fresh cranberries
- 1/4 cup Dijon mustard
- 1/2 cup sugar
- 1/4 cup orange juice
- 1 tablespoon apple cider vinegar
- Salt and pepper to taste

Instructions:

1. In a saucepan, combine cranberries, Dijon mustard, sugar, orange juice, and apple cider vinegar.
2. Bring the mixture to a boil, then reduce to a simmer and cook for 15-20 minutes, until the cranberries burst and the sauce thickens.
3. Season with salt and pepper to taste.
4. Serve warm or chilled with turkey, chicken, or pork dishes.

Mustard and Bacon Mac and Cheese

Ingredients:

- 8 oz elbow macaroni
- 4 strips bacon, cooked and crumbled
- 2 tablespoons Dijon mustard
- 2 cups shredded cheddar cheese
- 1 cup milk
- 1/4 cup butter
- 2 tablespoons flour
- Salt and pepper to taste

Instructions:

1. Cook the macaroni according to package instructions and drain.
2. In a saucepan, melt butter over medium heat. Stir in flour and cook for 1-2 minutes.
3. Gradually whisk in milk and bring to a simmer until the sauce thickens.
4. Stir in Dijon mustard and shredded cheddar cheese until smooth.
5. Add the cooked macaroni and crumbled bacon, stirring to combine.
6. Season with salt and pepper, and serve hot.

Hot Mustard Pork Tacos

Ingredients:

- 1 lb pork shoulder, cooked and shredded
- 2 tablespoons Dijon mustard
- 1 tablespoon honey
- 1 tablespoon apple cider vinegar
- 1 tablespoon soy sauce
- 1 teaspoon chili powder
- 8 small tortillas
- 1/2 cup chopped cilantro
- 1/2 cup diced onions
- Lime wedges for garnish

Instructions:

1. In a bowl, whisk together Dijon mustard, honey, apple cider vinegar, soy sauce, and chili powder.
2. Toss the shredded pork in the mustard mixture until well coated.
3. Heat the tortillas in a skillet over medium heat.
4. Fill each tortilla with the mustard-coated pork, and top with cilantro, onions, and a squeeze of lime.
5. Serve immediately.

Mustard-Cabbage Stir-Fry

Ingredients:

- 1 small head of cabbage, thinly sliced
- 2 tablespoons Dijon mustard
- 1 tablespoon sesame oil
- 1 tablespoon soy sauce
- 1 teaspoon rice vinegar
- 2 cloves garlic, minced
- Salt and pepper to taste

Instructions:

1. In a large skillet, heat sesame oil over medium heat. Add garlic and sauté until fragrant.
2. Add the sliced cabbage to the skillet and cook for 5-7 minutes, stirring occasionally.
3. In a small bowl, whisk together Dijon mustard, soy sauce, rice vinegar, salt, and pepper.
4. Pour the mustard sauce over the cabbage and toss to coat evenly.
5. Cook for an additional 2-3 minutes, until the cabbage is tender.
6. Serve hot as a side dish.

Dijon Mustard and Roasted Beet Salad

Ingredients:

- 2 medium roasted beets, peeled and sliced
- 2 tablespoons Dijon mustard
- 1 tablespoon honey
- 1 tablespoon olive oil
- 1 tablespoon red wine vinegar
- Salt and pepper to taste
- 2 cups mixed greens
- 1/4 cup crumbled goat cheese
- 1/4 cup toasted walnuts

Instructions:

1. In a small bowl, whisk together Dijon mustard, honey, olive oil, red wine vinegar, salt, and pepper.
2. Arrange the roasted beet slices on a platter and drizzle with the mustard dressing.
3. Toss the mixed greens with a bit of the remaining dressing and place them on top of the beets.
4. Top with crumbled goat cheese and toasted walnuts.
5. Serve as a light lunch or side salad.

Mustard and Walnut-Crusted Fish

Ingredients:

- 4 fish fillets (such as cod, haddock, or tilapia)
- 2 tablespoons Dijon mustard
- 1/2 cup chopped walnuts
- 1/4 cup breadcrumbs
- 2 tablespoons olive oil
- 1 tablespoon lemon juice
- Salt and pepper to taste

Instructions:

1. Preheat your oven to 400°F (200°C).
2. Spread Dijon mustard over each fish fillet, then coat them with the chopped walnuts and breadcrumbs.
3. Place the fillets on a baking sheet and drizzle with olive oil and lemon juice.
4. Season with salt and pepper.
5. Bake for 12-15 minutes or until the fish is cooked through and the crust is golden.
6. Serve with a side of roasted vegetables or a light salad.

Mustard Garlic Roasted Chicken

Ingredients:

- 1 whole chicken (about 3-4 lbs)
- 3 tablespoons Dijon mustard
- 3 cloves garlic, minced
- 1 tablespoon olive oil
- 1 tablespoon fresh thyme, chopped
- 1 tablespoon lemon juice
- Salt and pepper to taste

Instructions:

1. Preheat your oven to 375°F (190°C).
2. In a bowl, mix Dijon mustard, garlic, olive oil, thyme, lemon juice, salt, and pepper.
3. Rub the mustard mixture all over the chicken, making sure it's well-coated.
4. Roast the chicken in the preheated oven for 1 hour and 20 minutes, or until the internal temperature reaches 165°F (74°C).
5. Let the chicken rest for 10 minutes before carving.
6. Serve with roasted potatoes and vegetables.

Mustard Glazed Asparagus

Ingredients:

- 1 bunch asparagus, trimmed
- 2 tablespoons Dijon mustard
- 1 tablespoon honey
- 1 tablespoon olive oil
- Salt and pepper to taste

Instructions:

1. Preheat your oven to 400°F (200°C).
2. In a small bowl, whisk together Dijon mustard, honey, olive oil, salt, and pepper.
3. Arrange the asparagus on a baking sheet and drizzle with the mustard glaze.
4. Toss to coat evenly, then roast for 15-20 minutes or until tender and slightly crispy.
5. Serve as a side dish with grilled meats or fish.

Mustard and Apple Coleslaw

Ingredients:

- 4 cups shredded cabbage
- 1 apple, thinly sliced
- 1/4 cup Dijon mustard
- 2 tablespoons apple cider vinegar
- 1 tablespoon honey
- 1/4 cup olive oil
- Salt and pepper to taste

Instructions:

1. In a large bowl, combine shredded cabbage and sliced apple.
2. In a separate bowl, whisk together Dijon mustard, apple cider vinegar, honey, olive oil, salt, and pepper.
3. Pour the dressing over the cabbage and apple mixture, tossing to combine.
4. Refrigerate for 30 minutes before serving.
5. Serve as a refreshing side dish to complement grilled meats or sandwiches.

Mustard-Dill Marinated Cucumbers

Ingredients:

- 2 cucumbers, thinly sliced
- 2 tablespoons Dijon mustard
- 1 tablespoon fresh dill, chopped
- 1 tablespoon white wine vinegar
- 1 tablespoon olive oil
- 1 teaspoon honey
- Salt and pepper to taste

Instructions:

1. In a bowl, whisk together Dijon mustard, dill, vinegar, olive oil, honey, salt, and pepper.
2. Add the sliced cucumbers to the bowl and toss to coat evenly.
3. Let the cucumbers marinate for at least 30 minutes before serving.
4. Serve chilled as a side dish or salad topper.

Mustard and Herb Marinated Chicken Breasts

Ingredients:

- 4 boneless, skinless chicken breasts
- 3 tablespoons Dijon mustard
- 1 tablespoon olive oil
- 1 tablespoon lemon juice
- 1 teaspoon dried rosemary
- 1 teaspoon dried thyme
- Salt and pepper to taste

Instructions:

1. In a bowl, mix Dijon mustard, olive oil, lemon juice, rosemary, thyme, salt, and pepper.
2. Add the chicken breasts and coat them with the mustard mixture.
3. Marinate for at least 30 minutes, or up to overnight in the refrigerator.
4. Grill or pan-sear the chicken breasts over medium heat for 6-7 minutes per side or until cooked through.
5. Serve with a side of steamed vegetables or a salad.

Honey Mustard Salmon Burgers

Ingredients:

- 1 lb salmon, skinless and boneless, chopped
- 2 tablespoons Dijon mustard
- 1 tablespoon honey
- 1 tablespoon lemon juice
- 1/4 cup breadcrumbs
- 1/4 cup chopped green onions
- Salt and pepper to taste
- 4 burger buns
- Lettuce and tomato for topping

Instructions:

1. In a bowl, mix chopped salmon, Dijon mustard, honey, lemon juice, breadcrumbs, green onions, salt, and pepper.
2. Form the mixture into 4 patties.
3. Heat a skillet over medium heat and cook the salmon patties for 3-4 minutes per side, or until golden brown and cooked through.
4. Toast the burger buns and assemble the burgers with lettuce, tomato, and the salmon patty.
5. Serve with a side of crispy fries or a green salad.

Mustard and Apricot Glazed Ribs

Ingredients:

- 2 racks of baby back ribs
- 1/4 cup Dijon mustard
- 1/4 cup apricot jam
- 2 tablespoons apple cider vinegar
- 1 tablespoon soy sauce
- 1 teaspoon garlic powder
- Salt and pepper to taste

Instructions:

1. Preheat your oven to 300°F (150°C).
2. In a small saucepan, combine Dijon mustard, apricot jam, apple cider vinegar, soy sauce, garlic powder, salt, and pepper. Bring to a simmer and cook for 5 minutes.
3. Place the ribs on a baking sheet lined with foil. Brush the ribs with the mustard-apricot glaze.
4. Cover the ribs with foil and bake for 2.5-3 hours, until tender.
5. Remove the foil, brush with more glaze, and bake for an additional 15-20 minutes.
6. Serve the ribs with a side of coleslaw or roasted potatoes.

Mustard Spiced Roasted Sweet Potatoes

Ingredients:

- 2 large sweet potatoes, peeled and diced
- 2 tablespoons Dijon mustard
- 1 tablespoon olive oil
- 1 teaspoon smoked paprika
- 1/2 teaspoon garlic powder
- Salt and pepper to taste

Instructions:

1. Preheat the oven to 400°F (200°C).
2. In a bowl, whisk together Dijon mustard, olive oil, smoked paprika, garlic powder, salt, and pepper.
3. Toss the diced sweet potatoes in the mustard mixture until evenly coated.
4. Spread the sweet potatoes on a baking sheet and roast for 25-30 minutes, or until tender and slightly caramelized.
5. Serve as a side dish with grilled meats or a hearty salad.

Mustard and Chive Creamed Spinach

Ingredients:

- 1 lb fresh spinach, washed and trimmed
- 2 tablespoons Dijon mustard
- 1/4 cup heavy cream
- 2 tablespoons butter
- 1/4 cup chopped chives
- 1/4 teaspoon garlic powder
- Salt and pepper to taste

Instructions:

1. In a large skillet, melt butter over medium heat.
2. Add the spinach and cook until wilted, about 3-4 minutes.
3. Stir in Dijon mustard, heavy cream, garlic powder, salt, and pepper.
4. Continue to cook for 2-3 minutes until the sauce thickens slightly.
5. Remove from heat and stir in chopped chives.
6. Serve the creamed spinach as a side dish with roasted meats or grilled fish.

Mustard and Bacon-Sautéed Green Beans

Ingredients:

- 1 lb green beans, trimmed
- 2 slices bacon, chopped
- 2 tablespoons Dijon mustard
- 1 tablespoon olive oil
- 1 tablespoon balsamic vinegar
- Salt and pepper to taste

Instructions:

1. In a skillet, cook the chopped bacon over medium heat until crispy.
2. Remove the bacon and set it aside, leaving the rendered fat in the skillet.
3. Add the green beans to the skillet and sauté for 4-5 minutes until tender-crisp.
4. Stir in Dijon mustard, olive oil, balsamic vinegar, salt, and pepper.
5. Cook for an additional 2-3 minutes, stirring to coat the beans in the mustard mixture.
6. Sprinkle the cooked bacon on top and serve as a side dish.

Mustard and Onion Baked Potatoes

Ingredients:

- 4 large russet potatoes, scrubbed and pierced
- 2 tablespoons Dijon mustard
- 1 tablespoon olive oil
- 1 onion, thinly sliced
- 1/2 cup shredded cheese (optional)
- Salt and pepper to taste

Instructions:

1. Preheat your oven to 400°F (200°C).
2. Place the potatoes on a baking sheet and bake for 45-60 minutes, or until fork-tender.
3. In a skillet, sauté the sliced onion in olive oil over medium heat until caramelized, about 10 minutes.
4. Once the potatoes are baked, cut a slit in the top and fluff the insides with a fork.
5. Drizzle each potato with Dijon mustard, then top with the caramelized onions.
6. Optionally, sprinkle with shredded cheese and return the potatoes to the oven for 5 minutes to melt the cheese.
7. Serve as a comforting side dish.

Mustard-Maple Roasted Squash

Ingredients:

- 1 small butternut squash, peeled and cubed
- 2 tablespoons Dijon mustard
- 1 tablespoon maple syrup
- 1 tablespoon olive oil
- Salt and pepper to taste

Instructions:

1. Preheat your oven to 400°F (200°C).
2. In a bowl, whisk together Dijon mustard, maple syrup, olive oil, salt, and pepper.
3. Toss the cubed squash in the mustard-maple mixture until evenly coated.
4. Spread the squash on a baking sheet in a single layer.
5. Roast for 25-30 minutes, or until the squash is tender and caramelized.
6. Serve as a side dish with roasted meats or as a light fall-inspired meal.

Mustard-Cream Sauce for Roasted Veggies

Ingredients:

- 1/4 cup Dijon mustard
- 1/4 cup heavy cream
- 1 tablespoon olive oil
- 1 tablespoon lemon juice
- Salt and pepper to taste

Instructions:

1. In a small saucepan, combine Dijon mustard, heavy cream, olive oil, lemon juice, salt, and pepper.
2. Simmer over low heat for 5-7 minutes, stirring occasionally, until the sauce thickens.
3. Drizzle the sauce over roasted vegetables like potatoes, carrots, or cauliflower.
4. Serve immediately for a creamy and tangy addition to your veggie dishes.

Dijon Mustard and Mushroom Gravy

Ingredients:

- 1 cup vegetable broth
- 1/2 cup sliced mushrooms
- 2 tablespoons Dijon mustard
- 1 tablespoon butter
- 1 tablespoon all-purpose flour
- Salt and pepper to taste

Instructions:

1. In a saucepan, melt the butter over medium heat.
2. Add the sliced mushrooms and cook until softened, about 5 minutes.
3. Stir in the flour and cook for another minute.
4. Gradually whisk in the vegetable broth, then add Dijon mustard, salt, and pepper.
5. Bring the mixture to a simmer, cooking until the gravy thickens, about 5 minutes.
6. Pour over mashed potatoes, roasted meats, or any dish that would benefit from a savory mustard gravy.

www.ingramcontent.com/pod-product-compliance
Lightning Source LLC
LaVergne TN
LVHW081500060526
838201LV00056BA/2859